This Journal Belongs To:

HALAQA JOURNAL

BY MUSLIM JOURNALS

*This journal was crafted from the heart
with artful detail from us to you.
Your satisfaction is very important, so for any
issues with your journal please contact:
hello@muslimjournals.com*

"When a group of people assemble for the remembrance of Allah, the angels surround them (with their wings (Allah's) mercy envelops them, Sakinah, or tranquillity descends upon them and Allah makes a mention of them before those who are near Him."

-HADITH (MUSLIM)

My Halaqa Notes

DATE:

Halaqa Topic:

My Halaqa Notes

Halaqa Thoughts:

My Halaqa Notes

Halaqa Reflections:

Points That Stood Out For Me:

My Halaqa Notes

>>>————————————————————→

DATE:

Halaqa Topic:

My Halaqa Notes

Halaqa Thoughts:

My Halaqa Notes

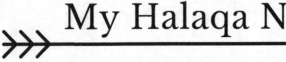

Points That Stood Out For Me:

My Halaqa Notes

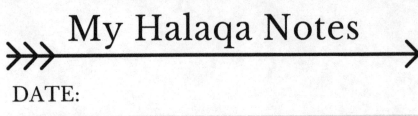

DATE:

Halaqa Topic:

My Halaqa Notes

My Halaqa Notes

Halaqa Reflections:

Points That Stood Out For Me:

My Halaqa Notes

>>>———————————————————————→

DATE:

Halaqa Topic:

My Halaqa Notes

Halaqa Thoughts:

My Halaqa Notes

>>>———————————————————>

Halaqa Reflections:

Points That Stood Out For Me:

My Halaqa Notes

DATE:

Halaqa Topic:

My Halaqa Notes

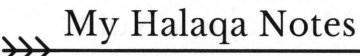

Halaqa Thoughts:

My Halaqa Notes

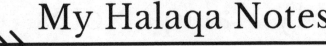

Halaqa Reflections:

Points That Stood Out For Me:

My Halaqa Notes

DATE:

Halaqa Topic:

My Halaqa Notes

Halaqa Thoughts:

My Halaqa Notes

Halaqa Reflections:

Points That Stood Out For Me:

My Halaqa Notes

DATE:

Halaqa Topic:

My Halaqa Notes

My Halaqa Notes

>>> ───────────────────────────────→

Halaqa Reflections:

Points That Stood Out For Me:

My Halaqa Notes

DATE:

Halaqa Topic:

My Halaqa Notes

Halaqa Thoughts:

My Halaqa Notes

Halaqa Reflections:

Points That Stood Out For Me:

My Halaqa Notes

DATE:

Halaqa Topic:

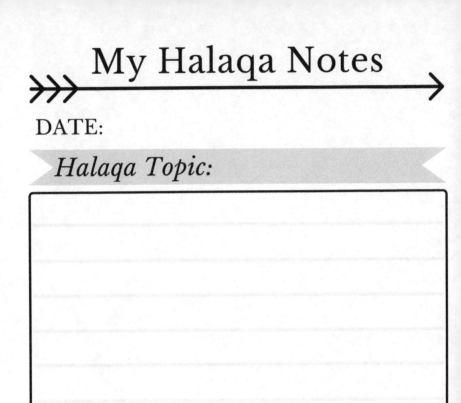

My Halaqa Notes

Halaqa Thoughts:

My Halaqa Notes

Halaqa Reflections:

Points That Stood Out For Me:

My Halaqa Notes

>>> ———————————————————————————→

DATE:

Halaqa Topic:

My Halaqa Notes

Halaqa Thoughts:

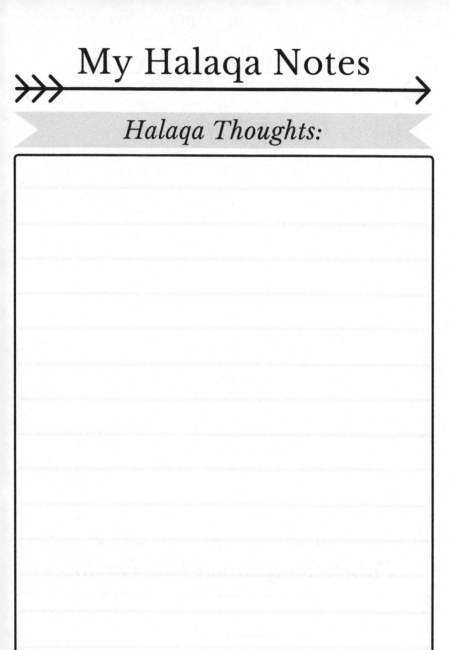

My Halaqa Notes

>>> ⟶

Halaqa Reflections:

Points That Stood Out For Me:

My Halaqa Notes

DATE:

Halaqa Topic:

My Halaqa Notes

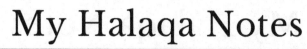

Halaqa Thoughts:

My Halaqa Notes

>>>———————————————————→

Halaqa Reflections:

Points That Stood Out For Me:

My Halaqa Notes

DATE:

Halaqa Topic:

My Halaqa Notes

Halaqa Thoughts:

My Halaqa Notes

Halaqa Reflections:

Points That Stood Out For Me:

My Halaqa Notes

DATE:

Halaqa Topic:

My Halaqa Notes

Halaqa Thoughts:

My Halaqa Notes

Halaqa Reflections:

Points That Stood Out For Me:

My Halaqa Notes

DATE:

Halaqa Topic:

My Halaqa Notes

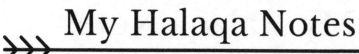

Halaqa Thoughts:

My Halaqa Notes

Halaqa Reflections:

Points That Stood Out For Me:

My Halaqa Notes

>>>————————————————————————→

DATE:

Halaqa Topic:

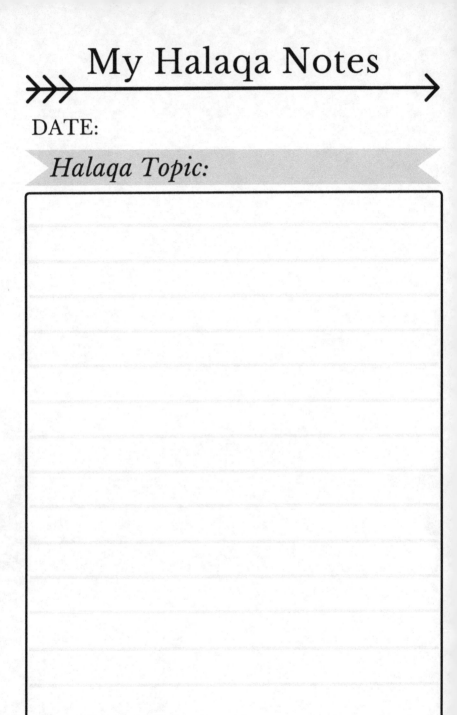

My Halaqa Notes

My Halaqa Notes

Halaqa Reflections:

Points That Stood Out For Me:

My Halaqa Notes

DATE:

Halaqa Topic:

My Halaqa Notes

Halaqa Thoughts:

My Halaqa Notes

Halaqa Reflections:

Points That Stood Out For Me:

My Halaqa Notes

DATE:

Halaqa Topic:

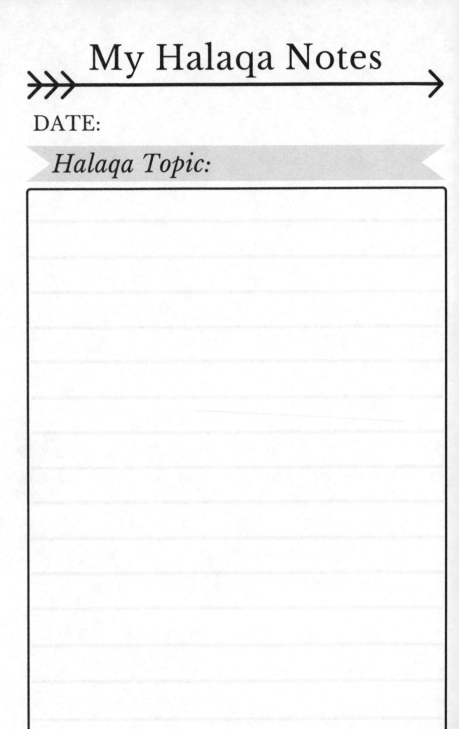

My Halaqa Notes

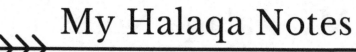

Halaqa Thoughts:

My Halaqa Notes

Halaqa Reflections:

Points That Stood Out For Me:

My Halaqa Notes

DATE:

Halaqa Topic:

My Halaqa Notes

Halaqa Thoughts:

My Halaqa Notes

Halaqa Reflections:

Points That Stood Out For Me:

My Halaqa Notes

>>>———————————————————>

DATE:

Halaqa Topic:

My Halaqa Notes

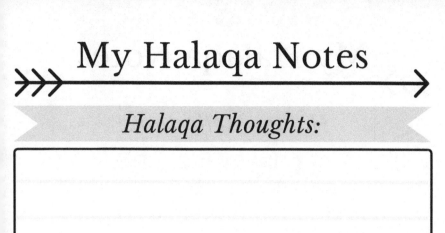

Halaqa Thoughts:

My Halaqa Notes

Halaqa Reflections:

Points That Stood Out For Me:

My Halaqa Notes

DATE:

Halaqa Topic:

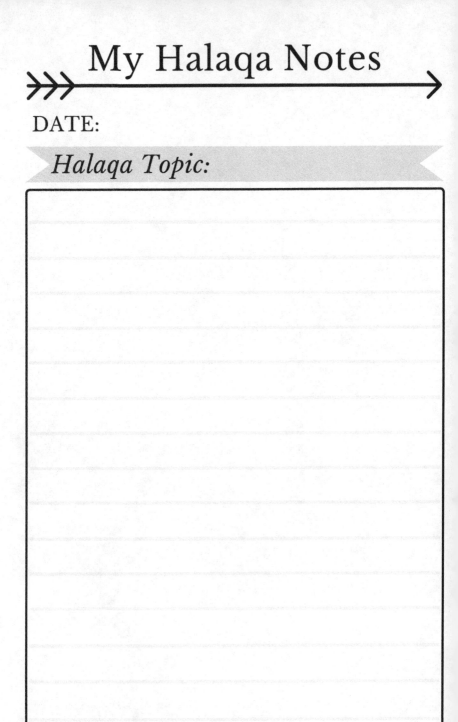

My Halaqa Notes

Halaqa Thoughts:

My Halaqa Notes

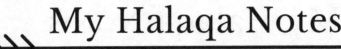

Halaqa Reflections:

Points That Stood Out For Me:

My Halaqa Notes

DATE:

Halaqa Topic:

My Halaqa Notes

Halaqa Thoughts:

My Halaqa Notes

Halaqa Reflections:

Points That Stood Out For Me:

My Halaqa Notes

DATE:

Halaqa Topic:

My Halaqa Notes

Halaqa Thoughts:

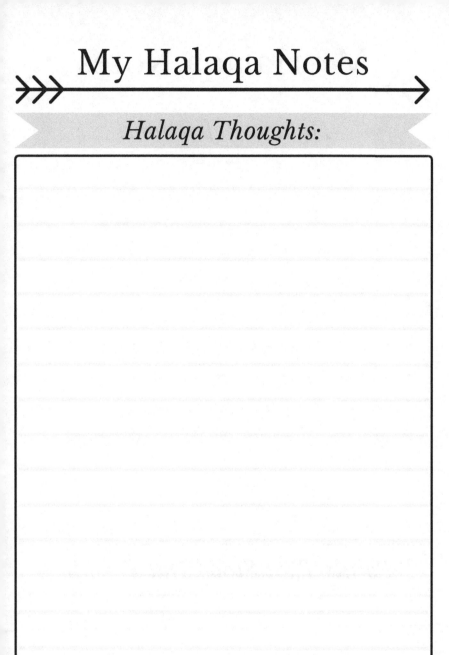

My Halaqa Notes

Halaqa Reflections:

Points That Stood Out For Me:

My Halaqa Notes

>>>————————————————————→

DATE:

Halaqa Topic:

My Halaqa Notes

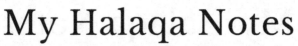

Halaqa Thoughts:

My Halaqa Notes

Halaqa Reflections:

Points That Stood Out For Me:

My Halaqa Notes

DATE:

Halaqa Topic:

My Halaqa Notes

My Halaqa Notes

Halaqa Reflections:

Points That Stood Out For Me:

My Halaqa Notes

DATE:

Halaqa Topic:

My Halaqa Notes

Halaqa Thoughts:

My Halaqa Notes

Halaqa Reflections:

Points That Stood Out For Me:

Notes

Notes

Thank you so much for purchasing the
Halaqa Journal.

If you liked this journal, please leave a review on
Amazon or share your comments on
www.muslimjournals.com

Jazakallah khair for spreading the joy!

Halaqa Journal
By Muslim Journals

Learn more about the author and get some freebies on our
website at www.muslimjournals.com. We offer many
more journals for men, women, teens, and kids.

Some of the options you will find include:

- Quran Journals
- Hadith Journals
- Dua Journals
- Salah Journals
- Sawm Journals
- Asma ul Husna Journals

- Shukr Journals
- Barakah Journals
- Niyyah Journals
- Halaqa Journals
- Ramadan Journals
  And many more!

Made in the USA
Las Vegas, NV
11 January 2024

84183164R00062